Lust

*To Noelle,
With poetic regard
Jade Nov '94*

Poems by
Jade Reidy
1990 - 1994

Gecko Press, London

LUST

Copyright © Jade Reidy 1994
All rights reserved

ISBN 0 9524067 0 5

First published by
Gecko Press in 1994
30B Stanmer St
Battersea
London SW11 3EG

Cover design by
Jade Reidy & Lolli Aboutboul

Illustration by
Janet Spriggs

Printed in Great Britain by
Antony Rowe Ltd, Wiltshire.

Thanks are due for time, inspiration and technology to-

Lolli, Mark, Gill, Colin, Anne, Barry, Joe John and Vince.

All poems previously unpublished except
Are You O.K. (Words From the Women's Cafe 1993)
and *Playmates* (Spring Collection 1993)

Introduction

I first heard Jade Reidy perform her poetry at a reading in Hastings in May 1993. I had arrived there a few days earlier and had given readings every night. Those few days had been frenetic and I wasn't in the mood on the last night but it was too late to get a train home to Edinburgh. I went on and grumpily went through the motions. There were some other perfomers but I'd had all the poetry I could take, and their work just washed over me. Then the MC introduced Jade.

She'd been sitting at the same table as me, her manner so reserved that I'd barely noticed her. When she got on stage she seemed to undergo some kind of metamorphosis.

The term 'performance poet' is used to describe just about anyone who stands up and reads their poetry out loud. But here was a performance poet in the truest sense, using the poem, her voice and her body to create a kind of theatre. On a bare stage in the back room of a run-down pub, she seemed to conjure up flickering images that made me feel as though I was watching the poems rather than just hearing them spoken.

Her final poem was one she had just written - "We Two". She'd perfomed all the other poems from memory, but this one was so new that she had to read it from the page. It didn't stop it from being the high point of her set. A terse, reproachful tale of one-sided friendship, it was Jade Reidy on her best form - intimate and personal without being cloying or self-referential. The poem was to resonate in my mind for the next few days. Discussing it on the way back to Edinburgh with David Scott, another Scottish writer, we agreed that we'd witnessed something pretty special. The following week, when a copy of "We Two" arrived in the mail, I was satisfied I hadn't imagined it all.

It wasn't to be the last time I saw her; later in the year she came to Edinburgh and was an impromptu performer at the Edinburgh Festival Fringe's "Beatniks to the Bar" event. Despite the number of highly acclaimed acts on there that night, her short set was one of the most memorable.

Since then, I've seen Jade perform in London and occasionally we have shared the same bill. My original opinion of her work is still the same. It has baffled me that she has chosen to publish so little of it, and so I'm delighted to see her finally put this book together.

She has wisely divided it into two parts. "In Performance", as the title suggests, brings together some raps and rants that, though well worth reading, suffer from the absence of body and voice - although it includes the sparse gorgeousness of "We Two". The second section, "In Private", is shorter and much better. Here she shows that she can write for the page as well as the stage, producing poems of quiet power that stand up on their own with as much presence as their creator stands at a microphone.

This book charts the evolution of a poet who is a throwback to the bards and minstrels of medieval times - a poet who takes poetry back to its oral roots without loss of seriousness, unlike the majority of "performance poets" who are simply stand-up comedians who use rhyme.

Many reading this book will probably be aware that Jade Reidy is a friend of mine. That's not going to stop me from enthusing about her poems. In fact, I'm proud that a friend of mine writes poems of such beauty and resonance.

-Barry Graham
Leith, Edinburgh
July 1994.

CONTENTS

In Performance

Playmates	11
Ninety degrees	12
Just another tourist	13
We two	16
Not all cycles are infinite	18
Taking reality by surprise	20
Related to silence II	22
Are you o.k.?	23
Fallen angels	25
No sexual solution to a failed revolution	27
She never loved to run	29
L.A.	31
Portrait of the poet as a young man	33
Home is where the heart is	35
Conversation	36
I can't come on a casserole	37
Lust, no labels	38
A bill of rights	40
He blames her for this	43
Self reliance	44

In Private

Fishing	49
The girl with the china doll	50
For Gareth	53
Related to silence I	55
Winter abroad	56
3.30	57
Faces in the well	58
Defenceless	59
As if leaving weren't enough	60
Dreamscape	61
Braces	62
Naked, for love	63

IN PERFORMANCE

Playmates

Music is the dance of life
and rhythm is the key
I have a good sense of rhythm
will you play with me?
Let my hands bow you firmly
finding low tones
of pleasure
fingers noting your valves
that pulse with my pressure
I want to palm your drum bum
slicing a slap that reverberates
pluck the strings
of your harp
slip my tongue seductively
over your mouthpiece
and suck in the air
ready to get high
notes
I won't come
to you in C sharp, B flat
or even major chords
just the rhythm pulsating
insistent
willing to touch
your music setting
my sex a dancing
as my fingers run
along the cadences of your keyboard

Ninety degrees

It was one of those days it was when even
thinking of doing something useful was useless
and it wasn't even depression or the asphyxiating
feeling that pollution was gonna get you before
fame had its chance but one of those days when
clothes clung like sticky hot tarmac the air so
heavy asthmatics were dying a day when you
roll down the blinds lay on the bed and spiral
out on a lazy wank hoping the neighbours will
put something sexy on the stereo to come to two
flats close by having a vinyl war one spins Carwash
on a tinny tiny music centre and you start to spurt
a little remembering Rose Royce sweaty nights
under strobe lights and the jocks in their silver
pants their straining packages then almost
before you can say Michael Jackson on acid
you feel the tension mounting opposite hey
dude huh huh crank up the volume and ACDC
explodes through shattered panes creaming
themselves on their own metallic destruction
and you want to stuff something up into every
orifice you've got cos baby it's a sound war
and reality's just another illusion to get off on.....

Just another tourist

I wasn't looking for romance when I learnt
the word *yassou* and greeted you with it
in the shop that day,
paying for Greek yoghurt and a jar of olives.
You asked me where I came from.
I made the fatal mistake of
wanting to know your name.
Alessandrou, this poem is for you

Subtly my morning ritual altered,
unwilling to enter your shop with
a face still creased by bad dreams,
tossed about by old memories, hair disarrayed.
I would seek refuge first in the sea,
in depths far kinder to swim,
returning wet to see you only then,
warmed by the light of pleasure
in the direct blueness of your gaze
that sought through my hesitant skin,
the way you made excuses to talk
and not just take my money,
rolling Turkish hash deftly beneath the counter,
the things you didn't say

I wanted your touch to distract me
from this old, incoherent pain,
a transient escape, no doubt
but to drown a few nights in
your sex would have been enough.
Just another tourist passing through,
it would have been easy to fuck with you
but I hate cliches and you
made no advances
except with your eyes

Smoking a spliff,
to escape the demands of a chattering head
you had earlier said,
we discussed the nature of village gossip
peoples' privacy being constantly betrayed -
proceed with discretion clearly conveyed

Monday night you tried to get me pissed
it was your birthday, you would insist
and hand me another glass of tequila,
but it was you who, stoned, fell asleep
on my shoulder, hand on my breast,
after teasing me for being too serious about life,
you who lived for the acquisition of drugs alone
that night I let your friends see you home

Word escaped and the next several
evenings at shop closing time
your aunt appeared,
fixing me with a look that said
"don't touch, he's going to marry
a nice Greek girl."
"I'll be back," you said on leaving to
drive her home into town.
I waited in the bar but
you never came

The word for sad is *merasi*,
you said, when I asked
the morning I was leaving
"but don't use it. Enjoy what's left."
I said I'd try. When I went in
later to say goodbye
you weren't there, your brother
was taking care of the shop.
So, was I just another ego trip?

My pride remains my passion
you will never read these words
but Alessandrou
this poem is for you.

We two

You left an hour after I arrived,
trailing phone numbers, instructions
and a bereft cat.
I wore your home for a year,
reading your books, sleeping in
the bed you used to make love in
and when my lover left,
feeling you were somehow more there
than she'd ever been

I only knew you then in labels,
landlady, journalist and now
backpacking tourist,
taken off for places I had travelled through,
sending postcards back
to tell the cat you missed him,
a photo in an envelope,
your long black curls hiding a thin face
that looked out at the world
and wanted to know more

You returned, your lover too,
he stayed aloof, cleaned windows
while you and I orbited each others' lives
like stars around a single planet,
trusting magnetism,
holding each others' truths carefully
more gently than our own.
Common ground viewed at
a distance fast diminishing

Or was it just that two women
born a week apart
must surely know where
the other has come from?
You were surprised at such swift intensity,
told me how you thought having a
woman lover must be like having
a best friend, only better.
I laughed at how simple things can seem
when viewed at a distance.

We talked through an entire Spring,
country afternoons laden with pollen,
saffron fields of rape eclipsing
a still convalescent sun.
I didn't notice at first that it was nearly
always me who came to find you, wanted more.
You began to leave the answer machine on.
"It's a question of trust," you said.
I pictured you cosy, coupled.
"One is only half as risky as two."

Undeterred by rejection
I kept phoning, willing to earn
what had once been a precious gift.
You sent me a Christmas card
this last year, from India,
wishing me peace and joy.
I didn't even know you had left England.
I cried then because I missed you
I still do.

Not all cycles are infinite

She's every old woman you dread in a laundrette -
the one who doesn't have any laundry of her own,
who watches you with beady eyes as you throw
your clothes in the only available machine.
"That one's not working, you know,"
and watches you just as close
as you haul 'em all out again with a groan.
"I've lived above here since 1924,"
she says while you wait.
You're gonna be late back for dinner now
and will they save you any?
Wishing you'd brought along a book
to escape into,
someone else's story
not hers again -
the list of operations and current ills,
her childrens' neglect,
a dead husband or two.
You're supposed to be kind to old ladies
but why me again?
As you smile and nod and say "that's nice,"
when it isn't

You get up to grab a free machine,
watching with one eye 'er try
to pull a small boy towards 'er lap.
He wriggles away from her knotty, needy fingers.

So she turns instead to the swirl of suds
the hot air and her captive audience
with their 'don't care' attitudes,
"Nothing's as clean in 'ere as was
since the last attendant left",
hauling 'erself up on arthritic legs
as another Autumn's wind
brings the leaves in.
Her broom wages war on a puddle of
grey soapy water and the leaves.
short-sighted, she misses a few.
You watch them play catch as catch can
in the breeze, thinking
'she can't keep up with the world
out there anymore'

Luckily not much changes over time
in a laundrette
except the fashion of the dirty washing
and it all goes round in cycles anyway,
catches 'er up periodically.
As you fish around in your pocket
for those 20p pieces
you thought you 'ad
you think about growing old and death
but only for a minute cos
after all, life's for living
innit.

Taking reality by surprise

I came here to write a poem
but even with a sky the colour
of deep well water and air clear enough
to drink on this liquid London day,
I can't seem to write about beauty.
The end of my pen's been chewed on
and I didn't do it,
the park smells of dog shit

"It's so hard to tell you how I feel
without hurting you,"
she belts it out, unselfconscious
across the grass with a wake
of little boys, parting, fighting behind her,
their voices rising disharmonious
in a now carbonated air
and the shit smell hits my nostrils again
at the same time as a stone in the back

Rolling over, I find the park awash
in budding male hormones, gloating
until a stone of my own
hits one of them in the penis.
"I'll take your face off for that,"
humiliated in front of three of his mates -
a sharp cockney accent,
they're all only about eight

"You started it."
I sound like one of them.
"Are you Australian?" the only White kid asks.
"We don't want your sort over here anyway."
The kid tosses easy words overheard,
understood by instinct alone,
just like 'nigger go home'
his father might have said

But now three Black boys dance
solidarity around this white face
and there'll always be someone
of another race who
wasn't born under a Union Jack.

Related to silence II

My lover's family came for the day
they're all straight
and we're out as gay.
We tucked the papers right out of sight,
pink and porn,
the poems we write -
our lives

My lover's family came for the day
they're all straight,
with silence we pay.
We talked of babies, bowling and beer,
gardening and shoe size,
not the fact that we're queer -
me and their daughter

My lover's family came for the day
they're all straight
and by the end of their stay
my skin had worn so thin from
stretching through the eye of their horizons
and still I didn't fit in -
nor want to

My lover's family came for the day
and none of us risked
what our hearts could say.
They went, we went to bed,
exhausted, disappointed and
leaving much unsaid -
lying between us.

Are you o.k.?

Dyke sex is safe sex
the woman said as
she went down on her lover
in their shared double bed
and anyway we're monogamous now,
avoiding the question of how
her love had made love
for the past twelve years
and with whom

She assumed that her partner
was a woman only woman,
an outright dyke and
everyone knew that was alright
and anyway it wasn't polite to
bring up the subject of sex,
especially not when doing it
conveniently avoiding her own
fling with a bisexual man
that other Spring

Besides, she thought, on that
same train of puritan logic,
face squashed between her lover's thighs,
we're not like those men who think
that ten different dicks in
a single week is still a few
short of satisfaction

She didn't want to know that
it can take only one
night of unrestrained fun
to become HIV too
for it's not who you are, lover
it's what you do.

Fallen Angels

Watch out, watch out, a bisexual's about
she's hanging round with lezzies like
she wants to be a queer
but someone said she fucks with men
so we don't want her here

She'll dump you for a man
when it suits her to be straight,
hiding in the het world of men
and power, giving all our
woman energy to the enemy

When she gets down
she puts it all around town
she just can't seem to choose,
continues to abuse
our safe definitions

I mean, how can you say
you're bisexual and gay?
Which one are you more really?
Who makes you come the most?
come on, come on, decide, decide
you can't hide all your life
behind that trendy label bi
so tell me, are you one of us
or one of them?

Don't worry dear, we've all been there,
this sitting on the fucking fence
it's just a phase you're going through,
we know you'll see the light quite soon
and then we'll just forget your heterosexual past.
You can't have your cake and eat it too,
so why don't you just stay with me
in our gloriously exclusive male community?
The company's simply the best,
Oscar Wilde, Langston Hughes and all the rest.
History's on our side of the fence
despite what anyone else may say
I mean, how can you be proud to be
anything other than strictly gay?

No sexual solution to a failed revolution

She said afterwards,
"I wanted to come too
and didn't."
In fact she didn't want him
to come in the first place
not there
not then
but the words to say
stop, take it out
never formed,
silenced by the part of his body
she'd sucked
fucked with
come to know as part of him.
It filled her now with a psychic pain
sticky
trickling down her thighs.
This was not a gift
only his power to take

She said later, convinced
"I want to be equal".
"You are", he replied lazily,
stretching out still
on the planet where his ejaculation
had propelled him
space age
new age
outrage

she is in a cage of shared history,
of grandmothers laying back
rigid in England's arms
mothers battered, raped
without any qualms,
the man who stuck a finger up
her three year old vagina
and those who said
"Forgive and forget,
it's all in the past now".
They crowd around her
set out to confound her
love for this man.
She can't hang out on his planet,
the earth needs her.

She never loved to run

A child with sad eyes and a crooked smile
carries a burden of secrets, lives in disguise
no words to speak, no-one to hear
she does not exist
yet she is full of fear

"It's for your own good,
daddy's doing this because he loves you
every daughter loves her daddy this way
but you're a wicked little girl
for tempting daddy so"

Sunrise almost never comes but when it does
she knows another night will follow day
and that there is no god,
only a monster in the shadows, cruel hands.
She is trapped in panic, walled in ice

"You were always such a happy child,
loved your dolls, good at school,
loved to run,
you never had many friends though,
a solitary soul"

She wants to run and run and run
so fast that he will never catch her
but still he comes in the night
puts a pillow to her face
and enters her with his lies

She is an angry woman intent on speech,
memories reclaimed despite their pain
and her own fear of his once held power
but the man who said he loved her so
tips his head back, laughs and denies

In her dreams she murders him a hundred
vicious, violent ways but revenge is never sweet.
Seeking freedom, she turns instead to
the child inside with the dry, sad eyes,
gathers her up in her arms and cries.

L.A.

In L.A. the rich are always on a diet.
They decided to let the poor see, just for a day
how hard it is to live that way.
"Come north," they said, "over the freeway divide
to our million dollar homes but don't come inside.
From the windows you can watch as we sate our desire
for avocados, jalapenos, lobster and papayas."

Those from the south sat and grew thin in the sun,
watching women with silicon tits anxiously having fun
while the dudes flexed their plastic pectorals.
Their anger grew like salsa, red and hot,
they wanted what it was the rich had got
but their idea for the welfare fed trash poor
was to be so thin that their bodies
began to consume its own flesh and black skin

It's hard to say how the fight began
but a black man went to the ground face first
and three cops finished what the one had started.
"You want an apology for a little restraint?
We had to. PCP made you psychotic and what
you don't have on you can always be planted, got it.
Your black brothers and sisters never complained,
they know it's legit. but just for you and the camera,
we'll get a jury in to prove it"

"Some viewers might find the following scenes
offensive."
on a twenty inch screen a white truck driver
gets beaten by a group of Black men.
Again and again this screen had shown
the beating of Rodney King and no
newsreader ever said a thing

South Central, justice only for the White
anger setting fire to Black lives as police
guard City Hall and Beverley Hills.
58 people die, all Black and Hispanic
as Bush plays with pronouns,
owning a problem that yesterday was 'theirs'
and rock stars know there's a buck to be made
in recording a song about peace, love and aid
'yeah let's have peace in L.A., peace in L.A.'
Justice stands, abandoned

South Central, a young Black kid
takes a looted gun and without telling anyone
he goes off to the airport, taking wild shots
at the bright, blinking lights of departing planes,
aiming for his own significant star.

Portrait of the poet as a young man

He's the one on the stage
in a roll neck jumper and tight black jeans,
a sheaf of well-thumbed A4 poems
acute descriptions of various one night scenes

After readings strangers buy him beer,
they ask to sit on his face
to existentialize (in verse of course)
back at their place -
women whose only pursuit of fame
is to be described, unclothed
in a poem of someone else's name

He could have been a rock star
or so he thinks
but he'd rather shag women
he can talk to over breakfast and drinks.
He's also got a list of ten best literary lays
which he'll definitely publish
one of these days

Unlike most men with no looks and little money
he doesn't fear ageing
knowing his status, his collected works
will keep schoolgirl hormones raging.
He's not above deception
he's got the literati fooled
he says he is a feminist
that sexism must be overruled

You can find him in the bookshop
signing copies, talking smart
while his wife types up his poems at home
and thinks they are great art

When the media ask him how it all began
he talks about his work as self-expression
what it means to be a man,
omitting the influence of a friend
who said it may not be well-paid
but being a performance poet
is a great way of getting laid.

Home is where the heart is

I made a home for you in my heart,
   it didn't have four walls
   but it had a door
   so you left.

Conversation

So I was talking about how the nuclear
family with its mortgage its 2 cars and
its 2.2 children is now a statistical minority
when you said you'd always wondered about this .2
imagining a pair of tiny legs trailing after dad
on the way to football of a saturday
swinging from the supermarket trolley
could be useful for the extra child benefit
after all it only needs a new pair of
sneakers every now and zen
no food no school books no expensive
dental work and no delinquent years ahead
so I said well it gives the dog something to chew on

I can't come on a casserole
A Vegetarian Epicure

My attention focuses on
the chickpea casserole
and you.
The food is delicious
but I'd rather spend all evening
looking at you,
only I'm afraid my foolish grin
will give me away

We sit close on the couch
finding excuses to touch,
me not finding the words to
tell you of the passion that's
taken over my reluctant mind,
waves of excitement lapping
and fantasies of
you with me with you

I wash my sheets in anticipation.
It rains for days and
they hang limp on a sagging line.
I see their weight as
the weight of my silence,
words suspended until sunshine
that could be a long
London time coming

I'm tired, I think
I'll wait till the weekend
finish bleeding
fast forward through Lovers II,
by then my sheets will be dry
by then I'll have
another excuse to let
you speak first.

Lust, no labels

You say we're all the same
gay and lesbian by name
butch in trousers, got no shame,
doin' it in the streets
in bars and clubs,
same sex sex, sure we got no shame
but there's more than one way
to play our game

Biker dykes do it with lots of lubrication
hiking dykes get off amongst the vegetation
right on dykes do it between meetings, over gin
closet dykes, guilty, call it a sin

Horny guys won't wait
masturbate, penetrate
safe sex, same sex
whip it good and latex

Shy dykes attempt it when another proposes
rich dykes entice you with dinner and roses
most dykes do it with their lover's best friend
S&M dykes don't care who it offends

Parliamentary gays do it in recess
drag queens and trannies prefer not to undress
gay priests are easy, there's always confession
the sisters of indulgence teach a strict lesson

Lust and thrust on the phone
you don't have to be alone
he talks about his big hard dick
and how he likes to suck and lick

Slip it in dildo, sleaze to please
the cool dykes thaw out with anti-freeze
celibate dykes rave on E all night
go home alone, turn out the light

Designer dykes do it with detachable dicks
bi girls like both cunts and pricks
cruisy dykes do it at the Hampstead women's pond
married dykes do it, how easy husbands are conned.

A bill of rights

Do I have the right
to take your hand in public,
to take your body in
the privacy of our own lust

Do I have the right to
fantasize you into someone famous,
to watch a porno movie
because it turns me on

Do I have the right
to prostitute my body, my art,
to make love to your partner
because it feels important

Do I have the right
to go to my woman lover and say
"I want your body"
after I've given you head

Do I have the right
to tell you that
my love for her makes
my love no less for you

Do you have the right
to pull your cock out
for a passing stranger if his eyes
say he wants that too

Do you have the right
at sixteen, to love without a law,
sex without secrecy,
equal rights, nothing more

Do you have the right
to whip him with his consent,
to hang weights
from his balls

Do I have the right
to ask if you are HIV
positive before I share
my body with you

Do I have the right
to say no if my past becomes
too painful to live in the
present moment of our sex

Do I have the right
to take my clothes off
in public without being
harrassed or raped

Do I have the right
to desire you with a dildo
to masturbate with it
in your presence

Do you have the right
to shave off all your body hair and still
be a man, to create your own cunt
and call yourself a woman

Do I have the right
to be a voyeur to all of this
a pleasure seeker
from every angle

Do I have the right
to pregnancy without a penis,
to feel erotic when my baby
sucks my breasts

Do your children
have sexual rights
do the disabled,
the elderly too

Do I have the right
to take responsibility for my own actions,
to be celibate and love myself
more than I can ever love you

Do I have the right
to commit a crime of passion
to walk away free
and what does the word yes mean?

He blames her for this

She goes walking with a man who
would be her tutor, would teach her what
lies at the top of a tall tower framed by
the setting sun. But there is no way up,
she says. He blames her for this and
begins to paint his own image in the grass
on which he tells her, 'lie, fuck with me'

Body of Christ, Jesus to a whore
you're not pure, are you? As he enters her
too easily, coming.
Withdraws and his cock falls off
followed by two breasts.
Find the virgin mary to restore, restore
but when they do, she's a whore, a whore

Pools of blood in a tampax temple
dipping his little round breasts,
her eight virgin arms thrust them
crookedly back onto his chest
but she holds his cock aloft,
waving and laughing
till her head falls off.

Self reliance

If the sky rained answers
I wouldn't mind getting wet,
if the earth erupted solutions
I'd live under a volcano,
if the sea washed waves of
explanations to the shore
I'd be a beach bum,
if the wind with its sweeping
gestures unravelled riddles
I'd be a kite caught up in its breath,
if the fire offered salvation
would I jump into it?

You know how it is
you go along awhile thinking
'Well, if this is life
I can handle it nicely, thanks',
and then you wake as if from dreams,
standing in the rubble of a new day
and there's nowhere to turn
but inwards.

IN PRIVATE

She winds her fingers around the wind

    and wills the roaring to cease.

Fishing

We are far from Wellington's concrete heat
these roads of tortured gravel
and dead opossum flesh,
sudden glimpses of a distant, pine-clad bay

Forced to sit on your lap,
my eyes fix on your thumb,
stranded on the dashboard, fish-hooked
remembering
your hand earlier too weak
to pull the outboard motor into life.
I sat ashamed of my little girl body
your anger nauseous
the smell of petrol

My mother's hands on the steering wheel now.
You shift in pain
and I am thrown;
shocked from its depths snags
another bloody barbed hook
from a different time
when your body - hard invasive hand
entered mine.

The girl with the china doll

Mama Papa rose up to meet her sky lover Rangi,
laid bare her mysteries,
her backbone of high mountain chains,
long arms of her rivers,
the volcanoes that were her breasts,
hot springs gushing forth between her thighs;
lulled by the hiss of salt ocean spray,
her legs wrapped around his mystical heights
and as she bore him down,
gave birth to the long white cloud
that became her secret. *

I

A young woman gives birth to a baby girl
in a land built on the ashes
of skin brown skull and bones.
Her body is not home anymore to a
silent slippery creature from another world;
shrinking back from its newborn screams
that echo her own unheard voice,
she becomes unable to remember
what she chooses to forget
and draws together her bloodied thighs
to slip behind the veil and disappear.

**Aotearoa* is the Maori name for New Zealand.
This translates as Land of the Long White Cloud

There are those who notice at times her absence
from life but do not comment
for they too are female and know how to absorb;
knitting information together like bones
they live out virtuous suburban lives
while a new consciousness births itself
on another continent in flower power.
The passion in their breasts is
cut out as cancer spreads,
bodies laid waste to the power of secrecy,
pain stitched up all over again

II

The baby girl begins to weave her own world of logic,
living in the cracks of a mirror image - one mother
split by the need for someone real to hold her;
good mother, bad child, her screams become
whimpers that enfold and engulf,
their sharp edges twisting in her gut
with every raised voice, every silent meal.
On her sixth birthday she is given a china doll.
Tirelessly teaching an unlearned love,
she feeds it, washes it, talks and talks to it
while glass eyes gaze back unblinkingly

III

The blood comes late, she hates its sudden spurts,
is prescribed the pill. Schoolgirl in Catholic grey
'No daughter of mine...' the chemist thinks,
undressing her with his eyes. Oestrogen-wise
she injects a line of travelling salesmen while
studiously etching schoolboy names on a pencil case
no-one guesses her other life, no-one tries.
She constructs herself in rock song lines
through the desert on a horse with no name
and a smile in disguise
her heart transplants to California, distant

From her sick bed a frail old lady
controls the woman who gave birth to
the girl with the china doll who
turns and flees the Long White Cloud
but still at night she dreams of smashing
the doll into a million tiny fragments.
By day her own fragility is not apparent to most,
they see her, a stranger from a land
of milk and honey who does not
return to its flaunted beauty.
Who can she tell she is afraid of disappearing?

For Gareth

It seems that I left you
although time says it wasn't that way.
You wanted marriage and kids then,
to come again in my mouth.
I was sixteen and didn't know what I wanted
but it wasn't that
strange stirring of memory

Your successor didn't last either. Blair in his
green van with mag wheels and opaque glass.
At a friend's party, her absent parent's bed
we slept and in the morning,
virgin sniffing the air,
she burst in, looking.
Too much brandy, not much lust
I made him come in my hand.
His mother always said I thought
I was too good for him

You write and tell me you went sheep farming
built a house, have two kids and an ex-wife.
Postmark, Palmerston North - a town where
the sheep are definitely sheep but the men
are not like I remember you, incurably romantic.
You ask me what's been happening in
the 4380 odd days since we last met,
I fill you in but can't get back
to the white house on the hill,
a bluegum tree that shivered in the night

You supply an image -
me in a red satin blouse with gold dragons
and a shark's tooth earring.
Did that girl leave you?
She is so hard to find
and I'm reading a poem that says
"All that I wanted then
is forgotten now, but you".*

*from Four Poems for Robin by Gary Snyder

Related to silence I

The skeleton in our family closet
wasn't white, she was brown.
Princess by birth, she wore
a cloak for a wedding gown,
lost her name to ours, gave birth,
such a shameful mistake
for a family of pakehas on the make

Now it has become trendy
to claim a Maori by blood,
not through bounty hunt
but by marriage stud.
Our skeleton was named
merely five years ago.
I discovered I have cousins
I don't even know

We don't share the same language
the same past,
what of our future?
Our shared knowledge is that
our families married into silence.

Winter abroad

This cold makes me homesick for heat
- a chorus of cicadas, hose pipe fights
and the sizzle of tarseal on weathered bare feet,
sensations of a half-remembered childhood

Saturday the sun's last rays bled red.
Summer died and froze over in English frost,
trees naked, balancing nests that
overflow the clean lines of limbs

I have flown my own nest in evergreen trees,
the safety of amniotic waters
to find a shivering kid left out in the cold
of memory

Strange how distance should prove
an easier route back.

3.30

She comes to collect her four year old.
The Green room is empty,
miniature chairs askew, underfoot.
Outside on the climbing frame
her daughter leaps, clocks her mother
and goes on playing, unconcerned

Two arms distract,
stretch out in front of her -
blind need, the sound of tears.
A scabby hand points to his knee
that might as well point to his heart,
hunger seeping out the scars of
a chicken pocked face

Compassion spurts from her breasts, painful
his arms now tight around her neck,
she gives what she can
inadequate food

Home, it is not his scarred face
she still sees but a small girl
who sits on chilled stairs at night
blue toes, white fear
and no-one comes.

Faces in the well

Here again in this boundless desert
willing non-existence,
a painless departure from pain
that circles like buzzards
    salivating
        over an almost dead
    childhood
glinting eyes already seeing the bones
      picked dry.
They cast their shadows over everything

Was last week then just a cruel oasis
drinking love like fire water
Autumn leaves splashed underfoot
and you underneath me
    in a wet
        wooded embrace
    I ran my
fingers over lines of age on your face
      watching it
relax into a seamless state of innocence

I cannot take you with me on this vast
desert journey across my past
must push you away
for several days to come
    fearful you
        would not stand
    the heat
there are no wells but salty ones of my
      own tears and
buzzards will feast on any dead flesh.

Defenseless

Wet October morning
'colder than last'
a woman behind me says
insulating herself with this knowledge
as I queue to cash a Giro

Wet October morning
it wasn't this cold last autumn
insulated by your skin.
You kept asking, Am I too heavy?
Ten stone is a weight
easy carried horizontally.
Your memory lies heavier.

As if leaving weren't enough

A bad acid trip would do no worse
at tearing me apart this unsought night
than your absence, love

Is a drug and I am its addict;
you gave just enough to keep my craving alive
never enough for satisfaction

Saying, this is just a thing
I'm having with you.
My mistake to think it had a name

I laid myself bare anyway,
the scars of past expectations,
hatching hope in a brittle egg

Today you scooped out its liquid centre
and said, I do love you
as you handed me the shell

How I wanted you to tell me that
all these months
but now it gives me no pleasure

I feel empty,
alone in a dying landscape of
perfectly rounded, hollow shells.

Dreamscape

The dead child is rattling in a double bass case,
skeleton attired to perform
in glittering beads and a velvet caress,
she is under wraps, percussive to the touch
"you're not dressed for the weather"
an old woman appears in front of me, pointing
merciless truth, she is right,
I am dressed for death
and, as always
unprepared

The dead children float upright on a river of tears.
They watch, anxious
for my precious bones to leave her musical coffin.
Laying her on a raft of my fears -
so heavy for one so slight,
it is me who jangles,
taking all my courage to stop
from screaming "no",
to push her out and watch
as she goes with the ones
who will take her home.

Braces

She smiles behind closed lips
prepared for his distaste
of metal on tongue on teeth
and when the dentist twists too far
the gums that bleed underneath

Closing her eyes, she waits
inviolate behind a plate of steel
railway tracks and a first kiss
a future promise of something
better than this.

Naked, for love

I stand before you
naked, raw,
the pain of my aloneness
overcoming fear of what
you might do to me
with this weapon called love

I would look for reasons to hate you
find ways to destroy this picture we have
painted together in sweat and desire
but I am learning to let such
madness die out in me
like a fire without a keeper

You inside me
stronger, harder, deeper.

Auotobiographical Note

Jade Reidy was born in Aotearoa (New Zealand) in 1962, where she lived until 1988. Since then, she has resided primarily in London, where she writes and performs regularly, in particular with Apples & Snakes and Survivors Poetry.